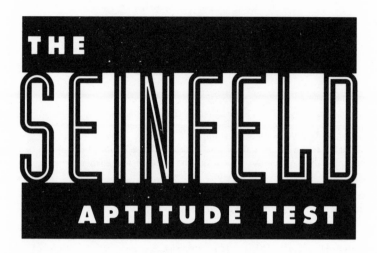

THE SEINFELD APTITUDE TEST

Hundreds of Spectacular
Questions on Minute Details
from TV's Greatest Show
about Absolutely Nothing

BETH B. GOLUB

A CITADEL PRESS BOOK
Published by Carol Publishing Group

A Citadel Press Book
Published by Carol Publishing Group
Citadel Press is a registered trademark of Carol Communications, Inc.
Editorial Offices: 600 Madison Avenue, New York, N.Y. 10022
Sales & Distribution Offices: 120 Enterprise Avenue,
    Secaucus, N.J. 07094
In Canada: Canadian Manda Group, P.O. Box 920, Station U,
    Toronto, Ontario M8Z 5P9
Queries regarding rights and permissions should be addressed to
Carol Publishing Group, 600 Madison Avenue, New York, N.Y. 10022

Carol Publishing Group books are available at special discounts for
bulk purchases, sales promotions, fund-raising, or educational purposes.
Special editions can be created to specifications.
For details contact: Special Sales Department, Carol Publishing Group,
120 Enterprise Avenue, Secaucus, N.J. 07094

Book design by Jessica Shatan

Manufactured in the United States of America
10 9 8 7 6 5 4 3 2 1

Library of Congress Cataloging-in-Publication Data

Golub, Beth B.
    The "Seinfeld" aptitude test : hundreds of spectacular questions
on minute details from TV's greatest show about absolutely nothing /
by Beth B. Golub.
        p.   cm.
    "A Citadel Press book."
    ISBN 0-8065-1583-X (pbk.)
    1. Seinfeld—Miscellanea.   I. Title.
PN1992.77.S4285G65   1994
791.43'72—dc20   94-20348
                                                          CIP

To Neal, Eileen, and Harvey.

CONTENTS

Introduction   ix

The Seinfeld *Aptitude Test* Scoring System   xi

LEVEL 1: Wuss Questions   3

MATCHING QUIZZES

    Family Trees   22

    New York, New York No. 1   24

LEVEL 2: This, That, and the Other Questions   29

MATCHING QUIZZES

    Edibles   47

    Oh, Boy!   48

    Potpourri   49

LEVEL 3: Tough Monkey Questions   53

MATCHING QUIZZES

    A.K.A.   72

    New York, New York No. 2   73

    Edibles, Too   75

LEVEL 4: Atomic Wedgie Questions   79

MATCHING QUIZZES

  New York, New York No. 3   98

  More Potpourri   100

LEVEL 5: Master of Your Domain Questions   103

MATCHING QUIZZES

  Answer Key   107

INTRODUCTION

It was a nothing that he knew too well. It was all a
nothing... Some lived in it and never felt it but he knew
it all was *nada y pues nada y nada y pues nada.*
—ERNEST HEMINGWAY, *A Clean, Well-Lighted Place*

So explains the format-bending premise and appeal of
TV's most innovative sitcom, *Seinfeld*. Each episode
is devoted to the trifling, picayune, and petty an-
noyances encountered by the show's characters on a daily
basis—looking for a parking space, missing rent-a-car
reservations, dilemmas in dating, anxiety about switching
barbers.

At the center of these misadventures is stand-up comedian
Jerry Seinfeld, who plays himself. Jerry is the nucleus of a
fabulous foursome consisting of best friend George Costanza,
ex-girlfriend Elaine Benes, and eccentric next-door neighbor
Kramer. Together they ponder the meaning of the mundane:
Jujyfruits, atomic wedgies, fake wood wallpaper, puffy
shirts, open-lipped kisses. The more insignificant, the
better. Clearly, *Seinfeld* has succeeded in transforming
nothing into *something* that audiences find endlessly fas-
cinating. For these minutiae-minded viewers, this book is the
ultimate diagnosis of their devotion.

*Place and character names not shown on the screen or listed in the credits are
spelled phonetically.

THE SEINFELD APTITUDE TEST SCORING SYSTEM

The *Seinfeld Aptitude Test* consists of 550 questions that are divided into five levels of increasing difficulty, culminating in the Master of Your Domain Questions. As a respite between levels, twist open a Snapple, double-dip a chip, and demonstrate your Seinfeldian savvy by tackling the ten (noncredit) topical matching quizzes. Afterwards, go back and see how you scored on the 550 questions.

CORRECT ANSWERS	HONORARY TITLES
0-140	**George:** You can't sustain a romance or hold a job. Not that there's anything wrong with that.
141-280	**Kramer:** You could have scored higher but were interrupted by an impending intestinal requirement.
281-420	**Elaine:** You're a tenacious professional who is test smart, but whose IQ seems to fluctuate widely.
421-550	**Jerry:** You're superman.

LEVEL 1

WUSS
QUESTIONS

1 To impress a woman, George passes himself off as
- Ⓐ a gynecologist
- Ⓑ a geologist
- Ⓒ a marine biologist
- Ⓓ a meteorologist

2 During a piano recital, Jerry places what object on Elaine's leg?

3 What did Jerry say about identifying a virgin?
- Ⓐ "It takes a trained eye and a patient soul."
- Ⓑ "It's not like spotting a toupee."
- Ⓒ "It's a God-given talent."

4 Kramer works in what capacity at the U.S. Open?

5 The Costanzas' house smells like which of the following?
Ⓐ Dandruff
Ⓑ Kasha
Ⓒ Mothballs
Ⓓ Cheap carpeting
Ⓔ All of the above

6 While waiting for a table at a Chinese restaurant, Jerry makes what wager with Elaine?

7 Where do Jerry's parents live?

8 Elaine's relationship with her writer-boyfriend ends because of his failure to use what kind of punctuation?
Ⓐ Periods
Ⓑ Question marks
Ⓒ Exclamation points
Ⓓ Colons

9 Where does George meet a woman who handcuffs him to a bed and steals his clothes?

10 Name the Pakistani restaurateur who opens a café across from Jerry's apartment?
Ⓐ Nehru
Ⓑ Babu
Ⓒ Mahmu

11 What candy does Kramer snack on while observing a surgical procedure from an operating-room balcony?

12 Who said, "I don't go for those nonrefundable deals...I can't commit to a woman...I'm not committing to an airline."?
Ⓐ Jerry
Ⓑ George
Ⓒ Kramer

13 Jerry's girlfriend poses as what to benefit from his dry-cleaning discount?

14 Jerry's bottom kitchen shelf is filled with what?

15 Where did George receive his infamous wedgie?
Ⓐ In the woods at summer camp
Ⓑ On the baseball diamond
Ⓒ In the locker room at school

16 What philosophy does George adopt in order to turn his life around?

17 Kramer enjoys going to the airport because
Ⓐ "it's a great place to meet women"
Ⓑ he's "hypnotized by the baggage carousels"
Ⓒ he "likes to stop at the duty-free shop"

18 In what infamous contest does the foursome participate?

NEXT QUESTION MUST FOLLOW ▷

19 Who withdraws first from the competition?

20 What is the name of the library investigator who tracks down Jerry for a long-overdue book?

21 A TV camera captures George sloppily eating what snack at a tennis match?
Ⓐ A foot-long hot dog
Ⓑ Cotton candy
Ⓒ Nachos and cheese
Ⓓ A hot fudge sundae

22 What article of clothing does Jerry make famous on the *Today Show*?

23 To what does "My boys can swim!" refer?

24 Kramer tells a couple that their baby daughter resembles what U.S. president?
Ⓐ Richard Nixon
Ⓑ Millard Fillmore
Ⓒ Harry Truman
Ⓓ Lyndon Johnson

25 Where are George's glasses stolen?

26 As a limousine passenger, how does Elaine avoid making small talk with the driver?

27 How does Elaine respond to Kramer's question,
"What do you say if neither of us is married in ten years,
we get hitched?"
Ⓐ "Sounds like a plan."
Ⓑ "Make it fifty."
Ⓒ "When chickens have lips."

28 What is Kramer's secret weapon for meeting women?

29 Mr. Seinfeld believes what has been stolen from him
at a doctor's office?

30 Jerry is unable to rid his car of what pungent odor?

31 Jerry is shocked by his date's dirty talk about what
piece of women's lingerie?
Ⓐ A bra
Ⓑ A teddy
Ⓒ A pair of panties

32 What famous baseball player befriends Jerry and
George in a locker room?

33 George anxiously awaits a phone call from whom at a
Chinese restaurant?
Ⓐ His mother
Ⓑ A prospective employer
Ⓒ His girlfriend
Ⓓ The president of NBC

34 Why does Kramer get banned from the fruit store?

35 Elaine berates a psychic for what behavior?

Ⓐ Using chemical pesticides

Ⓑ Smoking while pregnant

Ⓒ Wearing fur-lined boots

36 Newman tattles on Jerry for necking throughout what movie?

37 Kramer and a fellow stand-in play what game on the soap opera set to pass time?

Ⓐ Twister

Ⓑ Ink-a-dink

Ⓒ Pictionary

Ⓓ Rock, paper, scissors

38 According to Jerry, what are the four worst words in the English language?

Ⓐ "Make love to me."

Ⓑ "We have to talk."

Ⓒ "Your flight's been canceled."

39 What color is the defective condom George uses on a blind date?

40 Kramer gets a part in what famous director's movie?

41 Where does Newman live?

42 On an airline flight, Elaine misses the dinner service and finds that the only thing left to eat is

Ⓐ a bag of stale peanuts
Ⓑ a kosher meal
Ⓒ cubes of cheese
Ⓓ deviled eggs

43 Mr. Costanza gets George a job interview for what position?

44 George visits his mother daily during her hospital stay so he can watch (through the curtain) the nurses give her roommate
Ⓐ an enema
Ⓑ an IV
Ⓒ a sponge bath

45 A fellow health club member threatens to report George for what proscribed behavior?

46 Jerry's barber is entranced by what movie?

47 George claims that half of his high-school graduating class had undergone what cosmetic procedure?
Ⓐ Tattoo removal
Ⓑ Breast implants
Ⓒ Nose job
Ⓓ Liposuction

48 Why does Kramer's yogurt store venture fail?

49 Jerry makes a humorous remark to an elderly relative that greatly upsets her. She dies the next day. The remark concerns what animal?

Ⓐ A puppy

Ⓑ A pony

Ⓒ A kitten

Ⓓ A calf

NEXT QUESTION MUST FOLLOW ▷

50 Why does Elaine accompany Jerry to the funeral?

51 George saves a beached whale by removing what object from its blow hole?

52 Elaine believes that her boyfriend, who has the same name as a New York serial killer, possesses all of the following attributes *except*

Ⓐ he's good looking

Ⓑ he's a good shaver

Ⓒ he's a good dancer

Ⓓ he hasn't vomited in eight years

53 What designer steals Kramer's idea for a perfume?

54 How does Jerry get even with a woman who heckles him during an important comedy show?

55 What color shirt does George intentionally wear to a baby shower?

Ⓐ Red
Ⓑ White
Ⓒ Blue

56 Where does Jerry store his bicycle?

57 The NBC president becomes infatuated with Elaine after leering at
Ⓐ her firm thighs
Ⓑ her ample cleavage
Ⓒ her shapely derriere
Ⓓ her luscious lashes

58 Who uses the handle "Buck Naked"?

59 Elaine befriends an elderly woman but finds visiting her unpleasant because
Ⓐ the woman parades around her house naked
Ⓑ the woman has an unsightly goiter
Ⓒ the woman has bad breath
Ⓓ the woman is an incessant talker

NEXT QUESTION MUST FOLLOW ▷

60 Elaine's elderly friend reveals that she had an affair with what political leader?

61 As a model, what apparel does George wear to protect his hands?

62 George has a nonsexual crush on which of Elaine's boyfriends?

Ⓐ Tony, the rockclimber

Ⓑ Jake, the writer

Ⓒ Russell, the president of NBC

63 Who says "Giddee up!"?

64 Jerry is perceived as gay because he possesses what three characteristics?

65 Kramer believes he has seen what type of genetic mutation at the hospital?

Ⓐ A pig man

Ⓑ A snake lady

Ⓒ A half-man/half-woman

Ⓓ A dog boy

66 Jerry refuses to return what type of food to the grocery store?

67 Jerry, Kramer, and Elaine share the same complaint about George's baldness medication. What is it?

68 Elaine berates a women at a party for wearing what article of clothing?

Ⓐ A fur coat

Ⓑ Alligator shoes

Ⓒ A thong

69 Jerry and George pitch their idea for a sitcom to NBC. What is the pilot's premise?

70 What happens to Jerry's new air-conditioning unit?

71 Kramer is apprehended and fined for what misdeed in the Hamptons?
Ⓐ Impersonating a lifeguard
Ⓑ Indecent exposure
Ⓒ Lobster poaching

72 Where does Elaine host the baby shower for a college friend?

73 Jerry and George commandeer an airport limousine and discover they are en route to
Ⓐ a Knicks game
Ⓑ a political rally
Ⓒ a Metallica concert

74 Why doesn't Jerry attend Elaine's charity bachelor auction?

75 Upon returning from a trip, Mrs. Costanza discovers what article of George's on her bed?

76 Elaine's coworkers tease her with what nickname after seeing her Christmas-card photo?
Ⓐ Lolita
Ⓑ Nip
Ⓒ The Naked Spurs

77 Why does George write these names on his hand: *Matthew, Luke,* and *Paul*?

78 Elaine is interested in which piece of Jerry's furniture when he considers moving?
Ⓐ The bed
Ⓑ The coffee table
Ⓒ The couch

79 Upon landing at JFK, who does Jerry see from his window sprinting down the runway?

80 What engagement gift does the foursome purchase for the Drake and the Drakette?
Ⓐ A Laz-Y-Boy recliner
Ⓑ A big-screen TV
Ⓒ A lightweight camcorder
Ⓓ A boxed Neil Diamond CD set

81 In Jerry's lexicon, what is "sexual perjury"?

82 What magazine does Elaine take from the Costanzas' home to read on the subway?

83 Where does Jerry meet Isabel, the air-headed, sexy actress?
Ⓐ In an elevator
Ⓑ At an accident scene
Ⓒ At a doctor's office
Ⓓ At a flea market

84 Kramer and Mr. Seinfeld plan to recycle what for profit?

85 What strange character does Jerry befriend on the subway?

86 After disliking the sequel, George rents the original of what movie that brings him to tears?
- (A) *The Happy Hooker*
- (B) *Lethal Weapon*
- (C) *Home Alone*
- (D) *Smokey and the Bandit*

87 On a flight home, Elaine and Jerry sit in separate sections of the plane. Where does each sit?

88 To which character does "His buttocks are sublime!" refer?

89 At a bakery, Jerry and Elaine struggle over their pastry choice for a dinner party. What do they select?
- (A) A carrot cake
- (B) A Black Forest torte
- (C) A cinnamon babka
- (D) A napoleon

NEXT QUESTION MUST FOLLOW ▷

90 What treat does Jerry buy for himself?

Ⓐ A muffin

Ⓑ A cookie

Ⓒ A doughnut

91 Who steals a mannequin from a trendy clothing boutique?

92 In the Hamptons, George prepares a scrambled-egg breakfast filled with what?

93 Kramer uses what device to monitor George's hair regrowth?

Ⓐ A video camera

Ⓑ A ruler

Ⓒ A magnifying glass

94 A pen owned by the Seinfelds' neighbor has what distinguishing characteristic?

95 Why does Elaine break up with Keith Hernandez?

96 Kramer's portrait is purchased by an elderly, eccentric couple for what price?

Ⓐ $5,000

Ⓑ $50,000

Ⓒ $5

97 Why is George's car vandalized in a shopping mall parking lot?

98 Which of the foursome appears as himself in Jerry and George's NBC pilot?

99 George's date finds what Italian dish more satisfying than his lovemaking?
Ⓐ Linguine
Ⓑ Spumone
Ⓒ Risotto
Ⓓ Fettuccine

100 Why is Jerry rushed to the emergency room after attending a bris?

101 According to Jerry, George possesses all of the following attributes *except*
Ⓐ he's strong
Ⓑ he can bait a hook
Ⓒ he can log roll
Ⓓ he's fast

102 Who throws an electronic organizer out of a limo window?

103 Who said "I usually work naked a couple of hours a day. I cook naked. I clean naked. Naked! Naked! Naked!"?

104 Why is Jerry especially repulsed by a man's failure to wash his hands in a restaurant men's room?

105 What was Mr. Seinfeld's occupation?
Ⓐ Poultry inspector
Ⓑ Slipcover salesman
Ⓒ Menswear salesman
Ⓓ Funeral director

106 George's candor leads to a dream job doing what?

107 While in California, Kramer lands a small role in what TV sitcom?
Ⓐ *Blossom*
Ⓑ *Beverly Hills, 90210*
Ⓒ *Murphy Brown*

108 How does George's girlfriend Susan's family cabin burn down?

109 George becomes spastic when he thinks he swallowed what in the coffee shop?

110 Jerry is alarmed to find what in a girlfriend's medicine cabinet?
Ⓐ False teeth
Ⓑ A fungicide
Ⓒ A home pregnancy test kit
Ⓓ Crotchless panties

111 Why does Elaine spy on Jerry's girlfriend in the sauna?

112 What is wrong with George's new eyeglass frames?

113 What kind of shoes does Elaine own that Gail, the chef, covets?
Ⓐ Giovanni's
Ⓑ Boticelli's
Ⓒ Enzo's

114 What does Jerry's barber find on his nephew's living room floor?

115 Why is Elaine embarrassed when her date gets paged at a New York Giants game?

116 George's puffy winter jacket is made of what material?
Ⓐ Lycra-Spandex
Ⓑ A polyester blend
Ⓒ Gore-Tex
Ⓓ Orlon

117 Who said "Boy, these pretzels are making me thirsty!"?

118 Kramer visits the Cuban embassy to procure what?

119 Jerry is perplexed because his date won't try what dessert?

120 Elaine gets bitten by a dog
Ⓐ in a pet shop
Ⓑ at a nude beach
Ⓒ in a bakery
Ⓓ in an optical shop

121 What is Kramer's favorite recreational sport?

122 What gift does Jerry get for Elaine at an antique store?

123 What gift does George give to Elaine in appreciation for getting him a job in her office?

NEXT QUESTION MUST FOLLOW

124 How is the gift defective?

125 Which of the following is one of George's lifelong dreams?
Ⓐ To have thick, lustrous hair
Ⓑ To float down the Nile in an inner tube
Ⓒ To sleep with a giant woman

126 What causes Elaine's giddy behavior at Mr. Seinfeld's honorary dinner?

127 What ritual does Jerry perform six times a day?
Ⓐ He flosses.
Ⓑ He combs his hair.
Ⓒ He gargles.

128 Kramer begins his book tour with an appearance on what TV talk show?

129 What gift of Jerry's does Mr. Seinfeld throw in the trash?

130 Who does Elaine think is the most unattractive world leader?
Ⓐ Queen Elizabeth
Ⓑ Indira Gandhi
Ⓒ Golda Meir

STOP

FAMILY TREES

1 Cousin Jeffrey

2 Uncle Leo

3 Manya

4 Isaac

5 Mr. Seinfeld

6 Mrs. Seinfeld

7 Mr. Benes

8 Mr. Costanza

9 Mrs. Costanza

10 Mrs. Kramer

a Former condo association president

b Drinks Colt 45 in the nude

c Arm-grabbing, loquacious garbage can picker

d Leaves a rent-controlled New York City apartment for
the Phoenix sunshine

e Gruff-talking, well-known novelist

f New York City employee who watches the Nature
Channel

g Wears sneakers in the swimming pool and has to "get
the good spot in front of the good building in the good
neighborhood"

h Enjoys the heat and never uses air conditioning

i Elderly immigrant whose beloved pony was "the pride of Krakow"

j Nagging, shrill-voiced *Glamour* magazine reader who was hospitalized for a back injury

NEW YORK, NEW YORK No. 1

MATCH THE FOLLOWING LOCALES WITH
THE CORRESPONDING EVENTS.

1 Poppie's
2 Hunan Fifth Avenue
3 Gus's Smoke Shop
4 Hotel Edison
5 Royal Bakery
6 8173 Riviera Drive
7 Pete's Tavern
8 The Dream Café
9 NBC Studios
10 Joe's

a Jerry's vomit streak ends
b Elaine takes an IQ test
c Jerry, Kramer, and Newman go on a stakeout
d Jerry, George, and Elaine wait interminably for a table
e George's hand-modeling career is cut short
f Jerry refuses to try the chef's special
g George is handcuffed to a bed by a woman who steals
  his clothes

24

h Jerry and Kramer are banned from the premises
i Kramer sells Mr. Lippman his book proposal and a
wooden Indian
j Jerry and Elaine are stranded

LEVEL 2

THIS, THAT, AND THE OTHER QUESTIONS

1 What game does George play with the Bubble Boy?

Ⓐ Chutes and Ladders

Ⓑ Pictionary

Ⓒ Trivial Pursuit

Ⓓ Twister

2 What is Kramer's first name?

3 Elaine is in the bridal party of a lesbian wedding as what?

4 According to Kramer, all of the following are scams *except*

Ⓐ the Dewey decimal system

Ⓑ free-range chicken

Ⓒ one-hour Martinizing

Ⓓ the carpet sweeper

29

5 What is Jerry's last guess to recall a date's name that rhymes with a female body part?

6 Which of Elaine's cohorts has *not* seen her naked?
Ⓐ Jerry
Ⓑ George
Ⓒ Kramer

7 What happens to Kramer at Elaine's charity bachelor auction?
Ⓐ His derriere is pinched by an admiring woman.
Ⓑ He falls off the runway into the crowd.
Ⓒ He is sold to the lowest bidder.

8 Whose father wears sneakers in the pool?
Ⓐ Jerry's
Ⓑ George's
Ⓒ Elaine's
Ⓓ Kramer's

9 How does Elaine develop back trouble while staying with the Seinfelds?

10 Calvin Klein hires Kramer to model what?

11 After witnessing a bris, George reacts by
Ⓐ throwing up
Ⓑ fainting
Ⓒ breaking out in hives
Ⓓ breaking into song

12 Whose address and phone number does George use as a phony employment reference?

13 George claims he has no "hand" with which girlfriend?
Ⓐ The pianist
Ⓑ The accountant
Ⓒ The performance artist

14 Who is Kramer's chubby buddy and sometimes business partner?

15 John F. Kennedy, Jr., befriends which of Jerry's ex-girlfriends?

16 What does Jerry's cousin Jeffrey do for a living?

17 Who substitutes for Jerry's neighborhood car parker when he goes on vacation?

18 What figure in American literature does Jerry constantly compare George to?
Ⓐ Huck Finn
Ⓑ Biff Loman
Ⓒ Tom Joad
Ⓓ Holden Caulfield

19 Elaine is ejected from Yankee Stadium for wearing what article of clothing?

20 Jerry and Kramer witness what surgical procedure?

Ⓐ A splenectomy

Ⓑ An appendectomy

Ⓒ A vasectomy

21 How does George avoid taking an IQ test administered by his girlfriend?

22 Kramer poses as Elaine's new boyfriend so that she can break up with

Ⓐ her writer boyfriend

Ⓑ her psychiatrist boyfriend

Ⓒ her baseball player boyfriend

Ⓓ her artist boyfriend

23 What is Elaine's ex-roommate's occupation?

24 Jerry wears his watch on which wrist?

25 Elaine describes a couple's ugly newborn baby as looking like

Ⓐ a pekinese

Ⓑ a troll

Ⓒ Granny

26 What was George's first career on the show?

27 Elaine gets George a job in her office doing what?

28 How does Elaine escape from Crazy Joe Davola's locked apartment?

Ⓐ She kicks him in the groin.

Ⓑ She clubs him in the knee.

Ⓒ She sprays him with cherry Binaca.

Ⓓ She drops a bowling ball on his toe.

29 What video of George's is stolen from Jerry's glove compartment?

30 Who *always* snoops in other peoples' medicine cabinets?

31 Jerry buys an expensive suede jacket with what kind of lining?

32 According to George, what was the single most damaging experience of his life?

Ⓐ When he broke his parents' favorite statue

Ⓑ When he had his first sexual experience

Ⓒ When he received his SAT scores

Ⓓ When he saw his father naked

33 What is the name of the Pakistani-owned restaurant that opens across from Jerry's apartment?

34 Kramer envisions creating a cologne that smells like what?

35 Elaine meets a pediatrician in the Hamptons who uses what word to describe her beauty?
Ⓐ "Bitchin'"
Ⓑ "Radiant"
Ⓒ "Breathtaking"
Ⓓ "Scrumptious"

36 What ploy do George, Jerry, and Elaine utilize to get seated at a busy Chinese restaurant?

37 According to George, what famous news personality has had a nose job?
Ⓐ Connie Chung
Ⓑ Peter Jennings
Ⓒ Willard Scott

38 What is Kramer's apartment number?

39 How does Jerry get his watch back?

40 George's decorated bedsheets feature what animals?
Ⓐ Dinosaurs
Ⓑ Dalmations
Ⓒ Ducks

41 Why is Elaine mortified by her Christmas-card photo?

42 Jerry receives what defective birthday gift from Kramer?
Ⓐ A two-line phone

Ⓑ A mohair sweater
Ⓒ A Salad Shooter
Ⓓ A case of motor oil

43 Kramer romances a lesbian woman he meets in a video store who shares his passion for what sport?

44 How is George punished for having sex with a woman in his parents' bed?

45 What is Jerry's response to seeing George's girlfriend topless at the beach?
Ⓐ "Yo Yo Ma!"
Ⓑ "Boutros Boutros-Ghali!"
Ⓒ "Nice rack!"

46 What service people are working in the midst of Elaine's baby shower for a college friend?

47 After his apartment is robbed, Jerry is most distressed about which missing item?
Ⓐ His TV
Ⓑ His watch
Ⓒ His answering machine
Ⓓ His stereo

48 George sells his father's old clothes to a used clothing store. What defect do they have?

49 Kramer leaves what item in Jerry's stolen car that is, remarkably, returned to him?

Ⓐ His gloves

Ⓑ His golf clubs

Ⓒ His carpet sweeper

50 What is George's immediate response to seeing his girlfriend's nose unbandaged?

51 Why does Kramer leave New York for California?

52 George is announced by the doorman at the NBC president's apartment building as

Ⓐ Mr. Cabana

Ⓑ Mr. Bonanza

Ⓒ Mr. Cantstandya

53 How does Elaine discover that Jerry's girlfriend's breasts are real?

54 How is George's hand-modeling career cut short?

55 Name the woman who dates both Jerry and George at different times.

Ⓐ Marlene, the sexy southern cashier

Ⓑ Jodi, the masseuse

Ⓒ Noel, the concert pianist

56 Who creates a "written list" of excuses to avoid an annoying friend?

57 How many pairs of undershorts does George own?

Ⓐ 10

Ⓑ 20

Ⓒ 30

Ⓓ 40

58 What is Elaine's father's occupation?

59 According to Jerry, what did Gandhi consume before he fasted?

60 Kramer involuntarily convulses every time he hears the voice of what celebrity?

Ⓐ Mary Hart

Ⓑ Dr. Ruth Westheimer

Ⓒ Charo

61 George writes with which hand?

62 Mr. Seinfeld popularized what raincoat syle?

Ⓐ The chesterfield

Ⓑ The diplomat

Ⓒ The Prince Albert

Ⓓ The executive

63 Crazy Joe Davola attends the opera dressed as what circus character?

64 Who photographs Elaine for her Christmas card?

65 Kramer decorates his apartment with fake-wood wallpaper so it will resemble what structure?

Ⓐ A fort

Ⓑ A ski lodge

Ⓒ A shed

Ⓓ A log cabin

66 George's accountant girlfriend wears what eating utensil as a hair accessory?

67 What does Jerry's apartment cleaner steal from his apartment?

68 Jerry and Elaine visit the Seinfelds for what occasion?

69 George keeps what on his winter jacket because he thinks women find it attractive?

Ⓐ The price tag

Ⓑ A Dukakis pin

Ⓒ A lift-ticket

Ⓓ A name tag

70 To what does "They're real and they're spectacular!" refer?

71 Why does Elaine exchange her babka for another at the bakery?

72 George discovers a baldness cure developed by a doctor from what country?

Ⓐ Russia
Ⓑ China
Ⓒ Tibet

73 What kitchen implement does Kramer use as a backscratcher?

74 What does Jerry's "virgin" girlfriend do for a living?
Ⓐ She's a masseuse.
Ⓑ She's a closet organizer.
Ⓒ She's a lineswoman.
Ⓓ She's a performance artist.

75 Who calls George, "Georgie"?

76 According to Jerry, the whole concept of lunch is based on what food?

77 What happens to Elaine's sixty-six-year-old boyfriend right before she breaks up with him?

78 George unconsciously whistles what tune during a limo ride with neo-Nazis?
Ⓐ "Over the Rainbow" from *The Wizard of Oz*
Ⓑ "Getting to Know You" from *The King and I*
Ⓒ "If I Were a Rich Man" from *Fiddler on the Roof*
Ⓓ "The Party's Over" from *Bells Are Ringing*

79 What ingredient does Kramer like added to his Chinese food?

80 Who sneezes on the NBC president's lunch?

81 George, Kramer, and Elaine's macho boyfriend embark on which of the following disastrous expeditions?
Ⓐ Sky diving
Ⓑ Canoeing
Ⓒ Rock climbing
Ⓓ Spelunking

82 Why do Jerry and Elaine get stranded at a party on Long Island?

83 Jerry has a dispute with a girlfriend over what men's clothing commercial?

84 George ponders all of the following career alternatives after losing his real-estate job *except*
Ⓐ talk show host
Ⓑ projectionist
Ⓒ general manager of a baseball team
Ⓓ stunt double

85 Elaine's electronic organizer has what defect?

86 Which of the foursome prefers to be on the bottom during sex?

87 George and Kramer are late picking up Jerry and Elaine at a bakery because their car is blocked by a double-parker. The offender turns out to be

Ⓐ David Letterman
Ⓑ Joe Davola
Ⓒ Saddam Hussein

88 Why is George fired from his job at Elaine's office?

89 To what does "I don't have a square to spare" refer?

90 What is the name of George's high school gym teacher who constantly harassed him?
Ⓐ Mr. Seaman
Ⓑ Mr. Neiman
Ⓒ Mr. Heyman

91 Jerry is obsessed with what superhero?

92 Why does George have his parents' coffee table refinished while they're out of town?

93 What famous writer does Kramer thinks he meets in a sauna?
Ⓐ Dr. Seuss
Ⓑ Norman Mailer
Ⓒ L. Ron Hubbard
Ⓓ Salman Rushdie

94 Who repeatedly shrieks, *"S-t-e-l-l-a!"*?

95 What is George's customary order at the coffee shop?

96 Jerry intentionally throws away what gift from his parents?

97 What kind of fruit does Kramer eat whole?
Ⓐ A pineapple
Ⓑ An orange
Ⓒ An apple
Ⓓ A banana

98 Newman has a weakness for what type of sweet treat?

99 George has a public _____ phobia?

100 Why does Jerry's model girlfriend end their relationship?
Ⓐ She thinks his comedy act isn't funny.
Ⓑ She catches him picking his nose.
Ⓒ She finds his table manners offensive.
Ⓓ She thinks she's allergic to him.

101 What does George purchase at a roadside stand during his trip to the Hamptons?

102 Who said "You should have seen her face. It was the exact same look my father gave me when I told him I wanted to be a ventriloquist"?

103 Jerry, George, Elaine, and Kramer drive to a New Jersey shopping mall so that Kramer can purchase what for his apartment?

Ⓐ An air conditioner
Ⓑ A TV
Ⓒ A bed

NEXT QUESTION MUST FOLLOW

104 What does Elaine get at the mall?

105 George unknowingly has what stuck in his teeth during a failed job interview?
Ⓐ A poppyseed
Ⓑ A piece of spinach
Ⓒ A piece of dental floss

106 What issue sweeps Rudolph Giuliani into the New York City mayor's office?

107 Who paints Kramer's portrait?

108 Who has an allergic reaction to an article of Jerry's clothing?

109 How did George's sadistic high-school gym teacher intentionally refer to him?

110 While in L.A., Kramer is falsely arrested for
Ⓐ insider trading
Ⓑ indecent exposure
Ⓒ mass murder

111 What does George get on his shirt at a baby shower?

112 Susan's grandfather's dying words were
Ⓐ "Remember the Alamo!"
Ⓑ "*Semper fidelis!*"
Ⓒ "Cherish the cabin!"
Ⓓ "Live free or die!"

113 Jerry has a cutout of what racy sports car on his refrigerator?

114 According to Mr. Seinfeld, which impressionistic painter was nearsighted?

115 George's breakup with his "pretentious" accountant girlfriend causes her to
Ⓐ join a cult
Ⓑ commit herself to a mental institution
Ⓒ enter a convent
Ⓓ join the circus

116 Who's considered a "chucker" in basketball?

117 What video does Elaine borrow from Jerry that she returns two weeks late?
Ⓐ *Havana*
Ⓑ *Caddyshack*
Ⓒ *Rochelle, Rochelle*
Ⓓ *The Ten Commandments*

118 Kramer dashes off the subway to get what snack at a certain stop?

119 What secret does George claim he will take to his grave?
Ⓐ His first sexual encounter
Ⓑ His SAT scores
Ⓒ His inability to get into podiatry school

120 Who pays for George's therapy sessions?

121 Who said "I never tasted a cough medicine I didn't love"?

122 Crushed by Elaine's rejection, the NBC president leaves the network and joins
Ⓐ Greenpeace
Ⓑ the priesthood
Ⓒ the Peace Corps
Ⓓ the circus

123 George wears a trendy new suit to an interview and discovers it has what defect?

124 To which of Jerry's girlfriends is George referring when he remarks "A woman who hates me this much comes along once in a lifetime!"?
Ⓐ The toilet paper miser
Ⓑ The masseuse
Ⓒ The tennis lineswoman

125 What is the name of the nun who becomes infatuated with Kramer?

126 What morning show host appears as himself and interviews Jerry?

127 How does Jerry confirm that his car has been stolen?
ⓐ He contacts the police.
ⓑ He calls his car phone.
ⓒ He is told by Newman, an eyewitness.

128 What does George use for eyeware after his glasses are stolen?

129 While in the Hamptons, why doesn't Jerry's girlfriend partake in the big lobster dinner?

130 How tall is Kramer?
ⓐ 6 feet, 1 inch barefoot
ⓑ 6 feet, 2½ inches (minus his hair)
ⓒ Exactly 6 feet, 4 inches

STOP

EDIBLES

1 Chicken salad

2 Pretzels

3 Mini-Ritz crackers

4 Creamed corn

5 Roasted potatoes

6 Gyros

7 Kishke

8 A tomato

9 Babka

10 Lobster

a Kramer feels as loose as this after a massage

b Mrs. Costanza prepares this on special occasions

c Jerry, Elaine, and Kramer share this craving on the subway

d Hurled at George by one of Jerry's girlfriends

e Elaine's has a hair on it

f The exact opposite of what George regularly orders

g Kramer uses this as bird food

h These make Kramer "thirsty"

i Jerry uses this as a peace offering

j George urges his date to "go for it"

OH, BOY!

MATCH EACH NICKNAME WITH THE APPROPRIATE "BOY."

1 Bubble Boy
2 Butcher Boy
3 Aqua Boy
4 Cable Boy
5 Pretty Boy
6 Golden Boy
7 Fly Boy
8 Triangle Boy

a Jerry
b George
c Keith Hernandez
d Elaine's artist ex-boyfriend
e Obnoxious plastic-tent dweller
f Jerry's favorite old T-shirt
g The mohel
h Elaine's sweaty exercise companion

POTPOURRI

1 Would like to have "shoehorn hands"
2 Wears PABA-free sunblock
3 Observes coma etiquette
4 Almost attended barber school
5 Nicknamed the "little bulldog" in college
6 Has a weakness for Jujyfruits
7 Believes home package delivery should be prohibited
8 Is a bathroom stall man

a Jerry
b George
c Elaine
d Kramer
e Newman

LEVEL 3

TOUGH MONKEY QUESTIONS

1 At the taping of the pilot, Crazy Joe Davola leaps from the audience shouting
Ⓐ "Remember the Alamo!"
Ⓑ "Sic semper tyrannis!"
Ⓒ "Cherish the Cabin!"
Ⓓ "Live Free or Die!"

2 Where do Jerry and George get arrested for public urination?

3 Why doesn't Kramer carry a wallet?
Ⓐ He likes to borrow money.
Ⓑ He doesn't own one.
Ⓒ His osteopath says it's bad for his spine.

4 Who said "I prefer the company of nitwits!"?

5 According to George, which of the following acts constitutes a "binding social contract"?
Ⓐ Agreeing to help a friend move
Ⓑ Agreeing to loan a friend money
Ⓒ Agreeing to pick up a friend at the airport

6 What is the name of the coffee shop that the foursome frequents?

7 Jerry is reminded of what cartoon character by his date's annoying laugh?
Ⓐ Elmer Fudd
Ⓑ Donald Duck
Ⓒ Porky Pig

NEXT QUESTION MUST FOLLOW ▷

8 Because of her irritating laugh, Jerry is afraid to watch what movie with his date?
Ⓐ *Plan 9 From Outer Space*
Ⓑ *Beetlejuice*
Ⓒ *The Naked Gun*
Ⓓ *The Ten Commandments*

9 How does Kramer mispronounce the word *statue*?

10 An enjoyable rubdown by a masseur awakens what fear in George?

11 Kramer characterizes Jerry and Elaine's past relationship in terms of what presidential couple?
Ⓐ George and Martha Washington
Ⓑ Lyndon and Ladybird Johnson
Ⓒ Abraham Lincoln and Mary Todd

12 What is Mrs. Costanza's first name?

13 Why do Jerry and George take the tennis lineswoman to a party?

14 George spends his entire first visit with a therapist
Ⓐ discussing his childhood
Ⓑ telling humorous anecdotes about ex-girlfriends
Ⓒ arguing about the hourly rate
Ⓓ trying to unzip his jacket

15 Who tells George's large-nosed girlfriend that she needs a nose job?

16 Susan's father is outed when his relationship with what deceased novelist is revealed?

17 Elaine, her close-talking boyfriend, and the Seinfelds see what Broadway musical together?
Ⓐ *My Fair Lady*
Ⓑ *Cats*
Ⓒ *The Who's Tommy*

18 George gets fired from what volunteer job?

19 Kramer steals rubber gloves from a hospital supply room for what purpose?
Ⓐ Coloring his hair
Ⓑ Staining his floors
Ⓒ Washing his dishes

20 How do burglars gain access to Jerry's apartment?

21 What is unique about the design of Kramer's book?

22 According to Jerry, "phase two" of a relationship includes all of the following *except*
Ⓐ increased phone call frequency
Ⓑ extra toothbrushes
Ⓒ blood tests
Ⓓ walking around naked

23 Jerry and George compared their high-school gym teacher's rotten teeth to what food?

24 Kramer joins what well-known aquatic organization?

25 George's blind date reveals to Elaine that her head was on a _____ during sex?
Ⓐ hairbrush
Ⓑ copy of *Hustler*
Ⓒ hotplate

26 Why does George swap eyeglass frames with a blind man from the health club?

27 Elaine dates a mayoral aide to Mayor Dinkins whom she meets where?

Ⓐ At a yogurt store
Ⓑ At an optical shop
Ⓒ At a pet shop
Ⓓ At the health club

28 Jerry reenacts the notorious spitting incident that occurred outside Shea Stadium involving Kramer and Newman. What instrument does he use as a pointer?

29 Jerry agrees to switch George's girlfriend's answering machine tape before she can hear George's angry messages. What signal do Jerry and George employ to accomplish this?

NEXT QUESTION MUST FOLLOW

30 George becomes flustered and blurts out what wrong signal?

31 At dinner with Jerry, Elaine, and her father, George can't stop singing
Ⓐ "Memories" from *Cats*
Ⓑ "The Surrey With the Fringe on Top" from *Oklahoma*
Ⓒ "Master of the House" from *Les Miserables*
Ⓓ "They Call the Wind Mariah" from *Paint Your Wagon*

32 What is Jerry's apartment number?

33 Susan has a crush on what TV talk show host?

34 Kramer poses as a police detective to recover what stolen item of Jerry's?

Ⓐ A car

Ⓑ A TV

Ⓒ A statue

Ⓓ A box of raisins

35 After irritating an airport baggage handler, Elaine's suitcase gets intentionally routed where?

36 Jerry's model-girlfriend appears in an ad for what perfume?

Ⓐ Essence

Ⓑ Ocean

Ⓒ Mist

37 Kramer repeatedly uses what household implement to practice his golf swing?

38 How is George's last name mispronounced by a maître d' in a Chinese restaurant?

Ⓐ Cantstandya

Ⓑ Bonanza

Ⓒ Cartwright

39 What are Mr. and Mrs. Seinfeld's first names?

40 Kramer pretends to film a porno movie in Jerry's apartment and he playfully titles it

Ⓐ *Jerry's Private Lessons*

Ⓑ *Buck Naked Rides Again*
Ⓒ *Elaine Does the Upper West Side*

41 What is Jerry's destination on his subway trip with the gang?

42 Jerry compares a car rental agreement to which of the following historical documents?
Ⓐ The Declaration of Independence
Ⓑ The Monroe Doctrine
Ⓒ The Emancipation Proclamation
Ⓓ NAFTA

43 George yells "fire" in a crowded room during what event?

44 Mr. Seinfeld is afraid of what sound?
Ⓐ His pant legs rubbing together
Ⓑ A dentist's drill
Ⓒ Velcro

45 Who breaks a story that exposes Jerry as a gay man?

46 Elaine has a fear of what animals?
Ⓐ Dogs
Ⓑ Spiders
Ⓒ Squirrels
Ⓓ Carousel horses

47 George purchases a special "bereavement" air fare that entitles him to a discount when he produces a death certificate. Where is he planning to travel?

> NEXT QUESTION MUST FOLLOW ⟩

48 Why does Kramer split the cost of George's ticket with him?

> NEXT QUESTION MUST FOLLOW ⟩

49 In lieu of a death certificate, George presents what to the ticket agent?

50 What is the name of Jerry's boyhood friend who hounds him socially?

Ⓐ Larry
Ⓑ David
Ⓒ Joel

51 Who said "I'm going to slip him a mickey...it's like a movie!"?

52 Name the fictitious off-Broadway comedy George claims to have written when asked by NBC executives about his qualifications?

Ⓐ *La Cocina*
Ⓑ *La Sardine*
Ⓒ *La Cucaracha*

53 From what abandoned car part does Kramer create a coffee table for a girlfriend?

54 What is the name of the reappearing Chinese food deliveryman?

55 What overdue library book does Jerry, unknowingly, have checked out for more than twenty years?
Ⓐ *Catcher in the Rye*
Ⓑ *Tropic of Cancer*
Ⓒ *Lady Chatterley's Lover*
Ⓓ *Heidi*

56 Why must Kramer wear a garlic necklace and bathe in vinegar?

57 How does George obtain the NBC president's address?

58 Kramer concedes his attraction to what TV show hostess when his book tour gets canceled?
Ⓐ Katie Couric from the *Today Show*
Ⓑ Mary Hart from *Entertainment Tonight*
Ⓒ Sonya Friedman from *Sonya Live*

59 Jerry and George go to a mental institution to retrieve what?

60 George sells his scalped opera ticket to
Ⓐ a portly Asian man
Ⓑ Newman
Ⓒ the father of a friend

61 How does Kramer curtail his addiction to TV?

62 How does Elaine find a mohel for the bris of her friend's son?
Ⓐ She looks through the Yellow Pages.
Ⓑ She canvasses friends.
Ⓒ She visits kosher butcher shops.
Ⓓ She attends a B'nai B'rith luncheon.

NEXT QUESTION MUST FOLLOW ▷

63 As the godfather, what is Jerry's function at the bris?

64 George receives hot stock tips from whom?
Ⓐ Pensky
Ⓑ Boesky
Ⓒ Wilkenson

65 Jerry refuses to allow what food in his refrigerator?

66 What soap opera is Kramer addicted to?
Ⓐ *General Hospital*
Ⓑ *The Bold and the Beautiful*
Ⓒ *The Young and the Restless*

67 According to Elaine, people should be seated in restaurants based on what principle?

68 How does George attempt to gain the upper hand in his relationship with a concert pianist?

Ⓐ He plans to pay for everything.
Ⓑ He plans a preemptive breakup.
Ⓒ He plans to withhold sex.

69 Jerry appears on the *Tonight* show with what celebrities?

70 What is the title of the NBC sitcom pilot that Jerry and George cowrite?

71 What celebrity frequents Elaine's health club?
Ⓐ Pee Wee Herman
Ⓑ Tom Cruise
Ⓒ Woody Allen
Ⓓ John F. Kennedy, Jr.

72 Kramer photographs whom in a men's bathroom stall?

73 According to George, which of the following situations is a good "personality showcase" for him?
Ⓐ A job interview
Ⓑ A double date
Ⓒ A therapy session
Ⓓ A karaoke bar

74 Jerry has lunch with George's ex-girlfriend so he can retrieve what items George carelessly left at her apartment?

75 What is Elaine's father's name?

76 George quits his real-estate job after getting a memo prohibiting him from
Ⓐ making personal phone calls
Ⓑ using the boss's private bathroom
Ⓒ using the conference room for sexual activity

77 What does Kramer wear to dinner at the Costanzas' house?

78 In a reconciliation letter to Jerry, his artist girlfriend plagiarizes dialogue from what Neil Simon film?
Ⓐ *Barefoot in the Park*
Ⓑ *Plaza Suite*
Ⓒ *Chapter Two*

79 George gets into trouble for leering at whose under-age cleavage?

80 What does Kramer wear to the sting operation designed to trap Jerry's suspicious accountant?
Ⓐ A trenchcoat and sneakers
Ⓑ A burgundy velvet smoking jacket and dark slacks
Ⓒ A blue mohair sweater and shades
Ⓓ A single-breasted brown suit and a matching fedora

81 Jerry's dry cleaner rewards him with a permanent dry-cleaning discount for finding what lost item?

82 To whom does George plan to say: "You think I'm some sort of loser that likes to be abused and ignored...whose shirt can be ruined...without financial restitution!"?

Ⓐ An ex-girlfriend
Ⓑ The dry cleaner
Ⓒ A neighborhood bully
Ⓓ A coworker

83 What happens to the new suede jacket Jerry wears to dinner with Elaine and her father?

84 George believes he resembles what celebrity when looking at himself in the coffee shop's bathroom mirror?

85 Who leaves an anonymous, sexy message on Jerry's tape recorder?

86 Jerry's barber offers Newman free haircuts for a year (and a comb) if he will do what for him?

87 Elaine tries to impress married friends by claiming she once dated
Ⓐ an astronaut
Ⓑ a matador
Ⓒ a pole vaulter
Ⓓ a male exotic dancer

88 What does George model for his first hand-modeling assignment?
Ⓐ A watch
Ⓑ A ring
Ⓒ A pair of gloves

89 Who said "I've driven woman to lesbianism before, but never to a mental institution!"?

90 George's accountant girlfriend pilfers what items from the coffee shop table after breaking up with him?

91 How do Jerry and George resolve a dispute about a desirable apartment they both wish to rent?
Ⓐ They thumb wrestle for it.
Ⓑ They play rock, paper, scissors.
Ⓒ They choose for it.

92 Who puts a "kibosh" on Jerry?

93 The NBC president eats what food that causes him to become suddenly ill?
Ⓐ Sushi
Ⓑ Moo shu chicken
Ⓒ Pasta primavera
Ⓓ Franks and beans

94 George fails to land a job because he refuses to sample what food at the interview?

95 Jerry's drunken airplane seatmate leaves his unruly dog in Jerry's care. What is the dog's name?
Ⓐ Kasha
Ⓑ Farfel
Ⓒ Kugel
Ⓓ Bagel

96 Mr. Costanza has an extensive collection of what?

97 After her successful cosmetic surgery, Kramer takes George's ex-girlfriend where on their first date?
Ⓐ The golf range
Ⓑ The beach
Ⓒ The reggae lounge

98 What is the name of the old man who parks cars on Jerry's block?
Ⓐ Pete
Ⓑ Felix
Ⓒ Sid

99 What does George do at a meeting with NBC executives that causes Susan to be fired?

100 What beverage does George serve to the woman he's trying to seduce at his parents' house?
Ⓐ Prune juice
Ⓑ Decaffeinated coffee
Ⓒ A pink lady
Ⓓ A Slim-Fast milkshake

101 Jerry is scolded by a coffee shop employee for bringing what condiment from home?

102 Jerry and Elaine develop a signal at a party in case either of them needs to be rescued from a bad situation. What is it?

Ⓐ Toe tapping
Ⓑ Eye rolling
Ⓒ Head patting

103 What type of air-conditioning unit does Jerry get for his apartment?

104 George has an affair with Elaine's married friend, who is turned on by the phrase
Ⓐ "God bless you"
Ⓑ "Happy trails"
Ⓒ "Opaa!"

105 What college did both Jerry and George attend?

106 To whom is Elaine referring when she says, "It's so sad that all of your knowledge of high culture comes from Bugs Bunny cartoons"?

107 What is Elaine's middle name?

108 What is an "Enzo"?
Ⓐ A fruited pastry
Ⓑ A haircut
Ⓒ An abstract painting
Ⓓ An expensive Italian shoe

109 Jerry dates his comatose neighbor's girlfriend. Who threatens to expose their relationship once the neighbor recovers?

110 George compares his mother to an unattractive version of what 1960s sitcom character?
Ⓐ Aunt Bee
Ⓑ Hazel
Ⓒ Granny

111 Who said "Retail is for suckers!"?

112 According to Jerry, what act in a male relationship is the equivalent of going all the way?
Ⓐ Helping a friend move
Ⓑ Picking a friend up at the airport
Ⓒ Loaning a friend money

113 Jerry takes what item of Kramer's to the dry cleaner so he can benefit from Jerry's discount?

114 En route to Los Angeles, Kramer hitches a ride with all of the following *except*
Ⓐ a van full of hippies
Ⓑ a motorcycle rider
Ⓒ a truck driver
Ⓓ a Winnebago full of poodles

115 How does George's father punish him for damage done to his car in a mall parking lot?
Ⓐ He spanks him.
Ⓑ He requires George to pay for the damage.
Ⓒ He grounds him.
Ⓓ He persuades George to become his butler.

116 George bumps into his ex-girlfriend, Susan, at a video store where he is returning what foreign film?

117 Jerry and Kramer are patrons of what fruit store?
Ⓐ Joe's
Ⓑ Felix's
Ⓒ Dave's

118 What is the purpose of the foursome's trip to the Hamptons?

119 What does Kramer's heckling girlfiend do for a living?

120 George converts to what religion for a girlfriend?
Ⓐ The Church of Scientology
Ⓑ Armenian Reconstructionist
Ⓒ African Methodist
Ⓓ Latvian Orthodox

121 What politically incorrect gift does Jerry give Elaine that offends her Native American girlfriend?

122 Who said "Nobody takes better care of their hair. You could serve dinner on my head"?

123 How does George get discovered as a hand model?

124 What word does Elaine's subway admirer (and *TV Guide* fanatic) use to describe her beauty?

Ⓐ "Bitchin'"
Ⓑ "Mesmerizing"
Ⓒ "Exotic"
Ⓓ "Scrumptious"

125 Kramer is determined to reclaim what item that he lent to Jerry's comatose neighbor?

126 Keith Hernandez invites Jerry to see what movie?
Ⓐ *Glengarry Glen Ross*
Ⓑ *Honey, I Blew Up the Kids*
Ⓒ *JFK*
Ⓓ *Blackbelt II: Fatal Force*

127 Who is afraid of Elaine's temper?

128 Mr. Seinfeld created the idea for the _____ trenchcoat?

129 Why does Kramer miss his audition for the pilot?

130 All of the following events occur during George's courtship of Susan. Which one is the last straw for her?
Ⓐ Her family cabin burns down.
Ⓑ She gets fired from a lucrative network job.
Ⓒ She gets vomited on.
Ⓓ She discovers her father is a homosexual.

STOP

A.K.A.

MATCH THE FOLLOWING ALIASES WITH THE APPROPRIATE CHARACTERS. SOME CHARACTERS HAVE MORE THAN ONE ALIAS.

1 Peter Van Nostrand
2 Buck Naked
3 Dylan Murphy
4 Wanda Pepper
5 Joe Friday
6 Cal Varnsen*
7 Andre
8 Donald O'Brien
9 Martin Van Nostrand

a Jerry
b George
c Elaine
d Kramer

NEW YORK,
NEW YORK No. 2

MATCH THE FOLLOWING LOCALES WITH THE CORRESPONDING EVENTS.

---

1 The Regency
2 Papaya King
3 Revelations Antiques
4 Champagne Video
5 Pfieffer's*
6 Sky Burger
7 The New York Public Library
8 J & T Optical
9 Hunan Fifth Avenue
10 Sun Shine Cleaners

a George receives his second atomic wedgie
b A ravenous Elaine suggests this eatery
c Newman catches Jerry "necking"
d George meets a woman he romances at his parents' home
e Kramer gets George a discount
f George joins Jerry and the lip reader on their date

g Kramer's irresistible craving draws him here
h Jerry introduces Uncle Leo to his "wife"
i Kramer meets a lesbian he romances
j Elaine sneezes on NBC's president's lunch

EDIBLES, TOO

MATCH THE FOLLOWING FOODS WITH THE
CORRESPONDING DESCRIPTIONS.

1 Coffee
2 Bran Flakes
3 Navy bean soup
4 Ring Dings
5 Ketchup
6 Doughnuts
7 Bouillabaisse
8 A pear
9 Chocolate syrup
10 Milanos

a Mrs. Costanza's brassiere is stained with this
b A performance artist douses George's shirt with this
c Jerry eats these in a 25% variety
d It's what George considers pilfering off the dashboard of a police car
e Jerry and George argue over the cleanliness of this in front of a student reporter
f Kramer spots a famous baseball player dunking these
g Elaine feeds this to her convalescing boyfriend

h George believes it's sometimes used as a buzzword for "sex"

i Kramer prepares this for Jerry's visiting parents

j It's what George would bring to a dinner party

LEVEL 4

ATOMIC WEDGIE QUESTIONS

> NEATLY DARKEN THE INTENDED CIRCLE OR WRITE
> OUT YOUR ANSWER. USE A NO. 2 PENCIL.

1 What magazine is George reading when his mother catches him masturbating?

Ⓐ *Cosmopolitan*

Ⓑ *Glamour*

Ⓒ *Playboy*

Ⓓ *Good Housekeeping*

2 What was the name of the coffee shop in the real-life TV pilot, *The Seinfeld Chronicles?*

3 Jerry lives on what street?

Ⓐ West 81st

Ⓑ West 83rd

Ⓒ West 85th

Ⓓ West 87th

4 Kramer has gotten traffic tickets for all of the following offenses *except*

Ⓐ speeding

Ⓑ failing to yield the right of way

© no doors

® no rearview mirror

5 What phony company name does George use as a reference in order to get his unemployment benefits extended?

6 George claims he was singing what song when he broke his parents' favorite statue while using it as a microphone?
Ⓐ "Born to Be Wild"
Ⓑ "McArthur Park"
© "Hey Jude"
Ⓓ "American Pie"

7 What movie do Jerry, George, and Elaine plan to see after dining at a Chinese restaurant?
Ⓐ *Glen or Glenda?*
Ⓑ *Plan 9 from Outer Space*
© *Murder by Television*
Ⓓ *Attack of the Fifty-Foot Woman*

8 Joe Davola's apartment is covered with photographs of whom?

9 What is the name of Kramer's barber?

10 George refers to the "Eiffel Towers" as a fictitious
Ⓐ apartment complex where he stayed
Ⓑ book that he read
© bistro where he dined

11 What candy destroys Elaine's relationship with her hospitalized boyfriend?

12 Jerry discovers that Elaine is writing a script for what TV show?
Ⓐ *Blossom*
Ⓑ *Beverly Hills, 90210*
Ⓒ *Murphy Brown*

13 George purchases a painting by an artist who paints what single geometric shape?

14 Elaine fears she has contracted what disease after reading about its symptoms in a medical text?
Ⓐ Botulism
Ⓑ Hookworm
Ⓒ Lyme disease
Ⓓ Rabies

15 Why do Jerry and Elaine have difficulty understanding Kramer's clothing-designer date at dinner?

16 What is Kramer's mother's name?
Ⓐ Esther
Ⓑ Babs
Ⓒ Lucy
Ⓓ It has never been mentioned

17 Why does Jerry wear sunglasses to a banquet for his father?

18 What does George purchase at a flea market?
Ⓐ A hat
Ⓑ A pair of glasses
Ⓒ A shirt

19 While vacationing in the Cayman Islands, Kramer plays backgammon nude with what swimsuit model?

20 Jerry dates a beautiful Anthony Quinn buff but is disturbed by her driving demeanor because she is
Ⓐ a Sunday driver
Ⓑ a backseat driver
Ⓒ a hit-and-run driver

21 What does Kramer wear for his portrait sitting?

22 How much money does NBC agree to pay Jerry and George to write their TV pilot?
Ⓐ $4,000
Ⓑ $6,000
Ⓒ $8,000
Ⓓ $10,000

23 What fruit makes George amorous?

24 Who said "You don't have to worry about me, I won a contest!"?

25 Elaine's ex-roommate suffers from what malady?
Ⓐ Foot-in-mouth disease
Ⓑ Lyme disease

Ⓒ Epstein-Barr syndrome
Ⓓ Shingles

| NEXT QUESTION MUST FOLLOW ⟩

26 How did Elaine's roommate contract this disease?

27 Why does Jerry get audited by the IRS?

28 George tangles over what item with a shackled prisoner at the airport gift shop?
Ⓐ A magazine
Ⓑ A bottle of aspirin
Ⓒ A pack of gum

29 Kramer fancies what name for his firstborn?

30 What is Elaine's all-time favorite movie?
Ⓐ *Rochelle, Rochelle*
Ⓑ *Shaft*
Ⓒ *Lawrence of Arabia*
Ⓓ *Hitler: The Last Ten Days*

31 Name the health club to which the foursome belongs?

32 How does Kramer transport his girlfriend's severed toe to the hospital?
Ⓐ In a Ziploc bag
Ⓑ In a cigar box
Ⓒ In a Pringle's can
Ⓓ In a Cracker Jack box

33 Why does Elaine dislike sitting in the backseat of a car?

34 What chubby weatherman is on the cover of Mr. Costanza's missing *TV Guide*?
Ⓐ Mark McEwen
Ⓑ Al Roker
Ⓒ Willard Scott

35 What occasion brings Jerry to the Bubble Boy's house?

36 Elaine tries to remove Jerry's car's foul odor from her hair by washing it with what substance?
Ⓐ Clam chowder
Ⓑ Tomato sauce
Ⓒ Prune juice
Ⓓ Castor oil

37 The Costanzas live in what borough of New York City?

38 What gift does Kramer receive from an admiring nun?
Ⓐ Silly Putty
Ⓑ A jump rope
Ⓒ A box of animal crackers
Ⓓ A Slinky

39 Why does Jerry's barber feel betrayed by him?

40 How do George and Kramer resolve a dispute about who will get to keep a statue?

Ⓐ They play strip poker.

Ⓑ They play Ink-a-dink.

Ⓒ They thumb wrestle.

Ⓓ They play rock, paper, scissors.

41 What is the name of the clothing store where Kramer gets his apparel?

42 What legendary baseball player does the foursome believe they see at the coffee shop?

Ⓐ Micky Mantle

Ⓑ Joe DiMaggio

Ⓒ Ted Williams

Ⓓ Sherwin Williams

43 Why does George become briefly attracted to Elaine?

44 Where did Kramer originally get his beloved jacket?

45 Mrs. Costanza serves Kramer what Spanish dish for dinner?

46 Lamenting his breakup with Susan, George sings what song?

Ⓐ "The Most Beautiful Girl (in the World)"

Ⓑ "Achy Breaky Heart"

Ⓒ "Zum Gali Gali"

Ⓓ "Another One Bites the Dust"

47 Why does Jerry suspect his accountant may have a drug problem?

48 Where does George take his unemployment counselor's daughter on their first date?
Ⓐ A puppet show
Ⓑ Bowling
Ⓒ McDonald's

NEXT QUESTION MUST·FOLLOW ▷

49 What is the name of George's unemployment counselor's daughter?
Ⓐ Carrie
Ⓑ Lisa
Ⓒ Debbie

50 Where did Jerry and George originally meet?

51 Kramer sells his book proposal to what publishing house?

52 Jerry's vomit streak ends after how long?
Ⓐ 19 years
Ⓑ 8½ years
Ⓒ 14 years
Ⓓ 16 months

53 What is the name of Elaine's boyfriend who has the same name as a New York serial killer?

NEXT QUESTION MUST FOLLOW ▷

54 What other characteristic does her boyfriend share with the infamous mass murderer?

Ⓐ Both have curly brown hair.

Ⓑ Both are fluent in Italian.

Ⓒ Both are adopted.

Ⓓ Both play the castanets.

55 How many pairs of undershorts does George hope to own?

56 What is the complete title of Kramer's book?

57 Jerry's dog-sitting duties interfere with his plans to see what movie with Elaine and George?

Ⓐ *Mondo Trasho*

Ⓑ *The Projectionist*

Ⓒ *Glen or Glenda?*

Ⓓ *Prognosis Negative*

58 Why does Kramer get fired as a movie extra?

59 Jerry's last name is mispronounced by a policeman as

Ⓐ Seinfold

Ⓑ Steinfeld

Ⓒ Seinfield

60 How does Jerry's car get stolen?

61 Jerry, George, Elaine, and Kramer attend what opera?

Ⓐ *Phantom of the Opera*

Ⓑ *La Traviata*

Ⓒ *Pagliacci*
Ⓓ *Carmen*

62 How does George's mother injure her back?

63 What birthday gift does Jerry receive from Elaine?
Ⓐ A Water Pik
Ⓑ A Bette Midler CD
Ⓒ A pair of button-fly jeans
Ⓓ Nude Polaroids of herself

64 Jerry plots revenge against a laundromat owner for allegedly stealing money out of his laundry bag. What does he do?

65 What does George do to cover his nervousness when he calls a woman?
Ⓐ He takes a belt of whiskey.
Ⓑ He runs in place.
Ⓒ He speaks with an accent.
Ⓓ He eats an apple.

66 Elaine's mayoral-aide boyfriend is fired for adopting her idea for a campaign proposal. What is the idea?
Ⓐ The name tag proposal
Ⓑ The good government proposal
Ⓒ The parking meter proposal
Ⓓ The indecent proposal

67 What is George's middle name?

68 What brand of odorless scotch does Jerry keep in his apartment?

69 George suffers from what he thinks is a heart attack, but it actually turns out to be
Ⓐ tonsilitis
Ⓑ bursitis
Ⓒ gastritis

70 Why does Kramer's photograph appear in the Sunday sports section?

71 Elaine's ex-Met boyfriend has which of the following hobbies?
Ⓐ He's a race car enthusiast.
Ⓑ He's a Civil War buff.
Ⓒ He's a bee keeper extraordinaire.
Ⓓ He's a philatelist.

72 Why does the TV pilot get canceled?

73 How is George's car roof destroyed while parked in front of a hospital?
Ⓐ By a low-flying plane
Ⓑ By a sudden cyclone
Ⓒ By a patient leaping to his death

74 What is Elaine's shoe size?

75 Jerry and George purchase stock in what type of company?

76 Elaine hallucinates while fasting for what medical test?

77 What woman does Kramer claim he is going to marry?
Ⓐ A mumbling woman
Ⓑ A wheelchair-bound woman
Ⓒ A pious woman

78 What two other jobs has Jerry held besides being a comedian?

79 George reports to work at a company not knowing whether he was hired at the interview. What is his first assignment?
Ⓐ The Mackenzie proposal
Ⓑ The Tuttle memo
Ⓒ The Vandelay project
Ⓓ The Pensky file

80 Who said "For me it's a step up. It's like moving from Iceland to Finland"?

81 What is the name of George's concert pianist girlfriend?
Ⓐ Patrice
Ⓑ Susan
Ⓒ Noel

82 Newman and Kramer become partners in a business venture selling used

Ⓐ cars
Ⓑ clothes
Ⓒ records
Ⓓ appliances

83 Who is a great squinter?

84 According to Elaine, the perfect mode of transportation for her would be
Ⓐ a gondola
Ⓑ a stagecoach
Ⓒ a moped
Ⓓ a rickshaw

85 Where does Jerry's long-overdue library book finally turn up?

86 What year did Jerry graduate from high school?
Ⓐ 1970
Ⓑ 1971
Ⓒ 1972
Ⓓ 1973

87 What is Elaine's boss's name?

88 Kramer collides with what famous tennis player during a championship match?
Ⓐ Martina Navratilova
Ⓑ Monica Seles
Ⓒ Renee Richards
Ⓓ Steffi Graf

89 What is Elaine's ex-roommate's name?

90 Why is the foursome trapped in a shopping mall garage for hours?

91 Who is George's favorite explorer?
Ⓐ Pizarro
Ⓑ de Soto
Ⓒ Eric the Red

92 What is the Latvian word that describes Kramer's power over women?

93 According to Jerry, what was the original title of Tolstoy's *War and Peace*?
Ⓐ *War, What Is It Good For*
Ⓑ *Tug of War*
Ⓒ *Make Love Not War*
Ⓓ *All Is Fair in Love and War*

94 Why does Jerry compare Elaine's "acting" ability with that of Meryl Streep?

95 What is the name of Jerry's arm-grabbing Uncle?

96 Who leaves a piece of used Dento-tape on Jerry's dashboard?
Ⓐ George
Ⓑ Kramer
Ⓒ Newman

97 What homemade gift does Elaine's weird subway admirer give her at the Costanzas' house?

98 What is Jerry's favorite cartoon cable station?

99 To impress others, George uses the term *venetian blinds* to describe which of the following?
Ⓐ A rock concert he attended
Ⓑ A trendy restaurant he dined at
Ⓒ A book he read
Ⓓ A play he saw

100 What high school did Jerry and George attend?

101 What Mets ballplayer is finally implicated in the infamous spitting incident?
Ⓐ Roger McDowell
Ⓑ Mookie Wilson
Ⓒ Lenny Dykstra

102 Jerry and George pitch a storyline to NBC executives centering on what character?
Ⓐ A chambermaid
Ⓑ A butler
Ⓒ A gardener
Ⓓ A cook

103 How does Jerry finally rid his car of its pungent odor?

104 Who files a lawsuit against Elaine?
Ⓐ Crazy Joe Davola
Ⓑ Newman
Ⓒ Ping

105 George recognizes a homeless man on the steps of the New York City Public Library as who?

106 Kramer conceives of his book idea while
Ⓐ skiing
Ⓑ mountain climbing
Ⓒ playing backgammon nude

107 Which of the foursome did not appear in the real-life TV pilot, *The Seinfeld Chronicles*?

108 Kramer dates a woman who loves to scratch his back. Where does she work?
Ⓐ At the coffee shop
Ⓑ At the health club
Ⓒ At a tattoo parlor

109 What is George's suit size?

110 What is the name of George's unemployment counselor?
Ⓐ Mrs. Sokol
Ⓑ Mrs. Pensky
Ⓒ Mrs. Snyder

111 Elaine tells the NBC president she doesn't want to see him any more because
Ⓐ she's pre-engaged
Ⓑ she wants to play the field
Ⓒ she doesn't like television

112 George joins Jerry and his lineswoman date for dinner at what kind of a restaurant?

113 Elaine attends a Yankees game instead of honoring what previous commitment?
Ⓐ A cousin's funeral
Ⓑ Her boss' son's bris
Ⓒ A friend's baby shower

114 George has sex with his blind date in which room of his apartment?

115 Kramer tries unsuccessfully to approach what child TV star with his script?
Ⓐ Fred Savage
Ⓑ Mayim Bialik
Ⓒ The Fresh Prince

116 George buys Jerry tickets to what Broadway musical for his birthday?

117 Which of George's ex-girlfriends becomes a lesbian?
Ⓐ Monique, the graduate student
Ⓑ Susan, the network executive
Ⓒ Patrice, the accountant

118 Jerry carelessly leaves how much money in his laundry bag at the laundromat?
Ⓐ $500
Ⓑ $1,000
Ⓒ $1,500

119 Where does George move when he runs out of rent money?

120 Mr. Costanza is terrified of what animals?

121 Who jumps out of a second-floor window in Jerry's building?
Ⓐ Newman
Ⓑ Elaine
Ⓒ Kramer

122 Why does the "virgin" break up with Jerry?

123 Kramer gets a job as a stand-in on what soap opera?
Ⓐ *All My Children*
Ⓑ *The Bold and the Beautiful*
Ⓒ *General Hospital*

124 George is offended when the pilot script is negatively critiqued by
Ⓐ his mother
Ⓑ Newman
Ⓒ his therapist

h George does his Jose Jimenez impression
i George claims the bouillabaisse pot is used as a toilet
j Elaine barks, "Sauce me!"

MORE
POTPOURRI

1 Is lactose intolerant
2 Still has Brylcreem in the medicine cabinet
3 Not ready for the "responsibilities of a pretend marriage"
4 Finds yodeling relaxing
5 Freckles, so doesn't go to the beach
6 Thinks uncircumcised men look like Martians
7 Would institute the death penalty for double parking
8 Is fearful of "shrinkage"

a Jerry
b George
c Elaine
d Kramer
e Newman

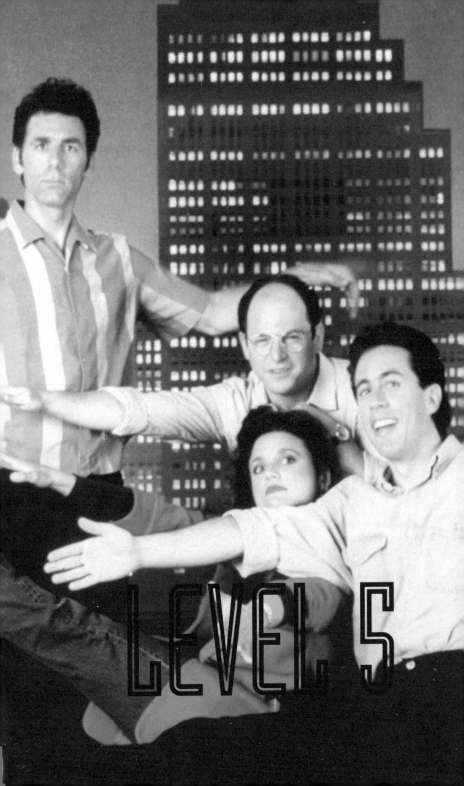

MASTER OF YOUR DOMAIN QUESTIONS

1 What is Jerry's exact address?

2 Jerry and George share a limo with members of what neo-Nazi organization?

3 Who is the creator of the Elaine mannequin-double?

4 Photos of whom are mounted on Jerry's refrigerator door?

5 What does George claim his SAT scores were?

6 After profiting from a stock tip, George invests in what type of a company based on a second tip?

103

7 What is the name of Kramer's offscreen buddy who works in a condom factory?

8 What is the name of the company for which George first worked on the show?

9 The Bubble Boy's father is a delivery truck driver for what chocolate-flavored beverage?

10 What is Kramer's phone number?

11 What year was Susan's family cabin built?
Ⓐ 1947
Ⓑ 1948
Ⓒ 1949

12 Joe Davola eerily refers to Elaine as what female operatic character?
Ⓐ Ursula
Ⓑ Nedda
Ⓒ Mercedes

13 A black-and-white photograph of whom hangs in Kramer's foyer?

14 Jerry's Pez dispenser is capped with what cartoon character?

15 What is the title of the book written by Elaine's father?

16 Jerry is arrested for public urination and invents what phony medical condition to excuse his behavior?

17 What is Elaine's IQ?

18 When Jerry is "outed," Mr. Seinfeld blames his wife for buying what article of girl's clothing for Jerry as a child?

19 What kind of lock does Jerry have on his front door?

20 Where does Elaine's sister live?

21 What is the Bubble Boy's name?

22 Kramerica Industries is what kind of business venture?

23 According to Elaine, Jerry's cousin Jeffrey looks like what animal?

24 A framed photograph of what ex-Mets baseball player hangs in Jerry's living room?

25 Kramer's book cover is what color?

26 What is the name of the fraudulent charity that Jerry contributed to that triggered his IRS audit?

27 What kind of computer does Jerry have?

28 What is the name of the company in which Jerry and George buy stock?

29 What volume in Mr. Costanza's *TV Guide* collection is missing?

30 What is the title of the screenplay Kramer tries to pitch while in L.A.?

STOP

ANSWER KEY

LEVEL 1

1 c
2 A Pez dispenser
3 b
4 As a ball boy
5 e (According to Jerry, it's a "potpourri" of all these odors.)
6 He offers her fifty dollars to go over to a stranger's table and take a bite out of an egg roll.
7 Somewhere in Florida
8 c
9 The subway
10 b
11 Junior Mints
12 a
13 His wife
14 Cereal boxes
15 c
16 He decides to go against his instincts and do the complete opposite of what he would normally do.
17 c
18 Refraining from masturbating
19 Kramer (after watching a nude woman in the apartment across the street)

20 Mr. Bookman
21 d
22 The puffy shirt
23 George's potent sperm
24 d
25 At the health club pool
26 She pretends to be deaf.
27 b
28 His jacket
29 His wallet
30 B.O.
31 c
32 Keith Hernandez
33 c
34 For returning a bad peach
35 b
36 *Schindler's List*
37 d
38 b
39 Blue
40 Woody Allen
41 Somewhere in Jerry's building
42 b
43 Bra salesman
44 c
45 Urinating in the shower
46 *Edward Scissorhands*
47 c
48 Because the yogurt is *not* nonfat as advertised
49 b

50 Because the deceased's husband is moving to Phoenix and Elaine wants to get her rent-controlled apartment.

51 A golf ball

52 c

53 Calvin Klein

54 He goes to her workplace and heckles her.

55 a

56 On the wall outside his bathroom

57 b

58 George

59 b

60 Gandhi

61 Oven mitts

62 a

63 Kramer

64 He's single, thin, and neat

65 a

66 Fruit

67 It stinks (which is repeated by all the characters)

68 a

69 "Nothing"

70 It falls out of the window because it's not properly secured and hits a dog on the street.

71 c

72 In Jerry's apartment

73 b

74 Because of a bad haircut

75 A condom

76 b

77 So he can pass his conversion test

78 c

79 Kramer

80 b

81 Lying about having an orgasm

82 An issue of *TV Guide*

83 a

84 Old raincoats

85 A naked fat man

86 c

87 Elaine sits in coach and Jerry sits in first class.

88 Kramer

89 c

90 b

91 Elaine (because the obscenely-posed mannequin looks just like her)

92 Lobster

93 a

94 It writes upside down.

95 He smokes.

96 a

97 Because he's parked in a handicapped spot.

98 Jerry

99 c

100 His finger is "circumcised" by a mohel.

101 c

102 A Russian writer whose book Elaine is editing

103 Elaine (while attempting to distract George's chauvinistic ex-boss)

104 He's the chef who is about to prepare Jerry's dinner.

105 c

106 He is hired as the assistant to the traveling secretary for the New York Yankees.

107 c

108 Kramer carelessly leaves one of his cigars burning.

109 A fly

110 b

111 Jerry wants Elaine to find out if she's had breast augmentation.

112 They're ladies' glasses from the Gloria Vanderbilt Collection.

113 b

114 Snippings of Jerry's hair

115 Her boyfriend has the same name as that of an infamous New York serial killer.

116 c

117 Kramer (It was his only line of dialogue in a movie).

118 More Cuban cigars

119 Apple pie

120 d

121 Golf

122 A wooden cigar-store Indian

123 A cashmere sweater

124 It has a red dot on it.

125 c

126 Overmedication on muscle relaxants

127 c

128 *Live With Regis and Kathie Lee*

129 A Velcro wallet

130 c

Family Trees

1 f
2 c
3 i
4 d
5 a
6 h
7 e
8 g
9 j
10 b

New York, New York No. 1

1 f
2 d
3 i
4 g
5 a
6 j
7 c
8 b
9 e
10 h

LEVEL 2

1 c
2 It's never been mentioned.

3 The best man
4 b
5 Dolores
6 b
7 b
8 b
9 She sleeps on a Hide-A-Bed that has a protruding bar.
10 His line of underwear
11 b
12 Jerry's
13 a
14 Newman
15 Marla, the "virgin"
16 He works for the New York City Parks Department.
17 George
18 b
19 An Orioles baseball cap that she refuses to remove
20 a
21 He has Elaine take it for him (by passing it out to her through his girlfriend's bedroom window).
22 b
23 She's a waitress-actress
24 His left wrist
25 a
26 He was a real-estate broker.
27 Working as a proofreader
28 c
29 *Rochelle, Rochelle*
30 Kramer

31 A pink, candy-striped lining

32 a and d

33 The Dream Café

34 The beach

35 c

36 Elaine tries to slip the maître d' a twenty-dollar bribe.

37 b

38 5B

39 He buys it back from Uncle Leo.

40 a

41 Her nipple is exposed.

42 a

43 Golf

44 His father grounds him.

45 b

46 Cable TV installers

47 c

48 They are moth-ridden.

49 a

50 He faints.

51 Because Jerry revokes his key privileges

52 b

53 She accidentally bumps into her in the sauna.

54 He is pushed into a hot iron and burns his hands.

55 a

56 Jerry

57 d

58 He's a famous writer.

59 Triscuits

60 a

61 He is a lefty.

62 d

63 A clown

64 Kramer

65 b and d

66 Chopsticks

67 A statue

68 Mr. Seinfeld is being honored at a dinner as the outgoing president of the condo association.

69 c

70 The authenticity of Jerry's girlfriend's breasts

71 It has a hair on it.

72 b

73 A spatula

74 b

75 George's mother

76 Tuna

77 He suffers a stroke.

78 c

79 Extra MSG

80 Elaine

81 c

82 George gets lucky with a woman from his office and drives home with her.

83 Levi's cotton Dockers

84 d

85 An alarm that doesn't shut off

86 Kramer

87 c

88 He had sex on his desk with the cleaning lady.

89 Toilet paper

90 c

91 Superman

92 Jerry carelessly leaves his mug on the table, which makes a ring.

93 d

94 Elaine

95 Tuna on toast

96 A watch

97 c

98 Drake's Coffee Cake

99 Bathroom

100 b

101 Tomatoes

102 George (describing his girlfriend's reaction to his confession that he cheated on the IQ test she administered)

103 a

104 Two goldfish

105 b

106 His campaign pledge to investigate the nonfat yogurt scandal

107 Jerry's artist-girlfriend, Nina

108 His accountant

109 "Can't-stand-ya"

110 c (He is mistaken for a serial killer known as the "Smog Strangler.")

111 Chocolate cake

112 c

113 A Porsche
114 Monet
115 b
116 George
117 a
118 A gyro sandwich
119 b
120 His mother
121 George (to his date)
122 a
123 The fabric rubs between his thighs and produces a *swoosh* like sound
124 b
125 Sister Roberta
126 Bryant Gumbel
127 b
128 Prescription swimming goggles
129 She keeps kosher.
130 b

Edibles

1 f
2 h
3 g
4 a
5 b
6 c
7 i
8 d

9 e
10 j

Oh, Boy!

1 e
2 g
3 b
4 a
5 c
6 f
7 h (Jerry dubs him this because he's a pilot.)
8 d

Potpourri

1 d
2 b
3 a
4 e
5 b
6 c
7 d
8 b

LEVEL 3

1 b
2 In a parking garage
3 c
4 Jerry (expressing his reluctance to have dinner with Elaine's intellectually intimidating father)

5 c

6 Monk's

7 a

8 c

9 "Statute"

10 That he may have homosexual tendencies

11 c

12 Estelle

13 For her lip-reading skills

14 d

15 Kramer

16 John Cheever

17 a

18 Volunteering to spend time with the elderly

19 b

20 Kramer leaves the door open.

21 The book has fold-out legs and turns into a coffee table.

22 c

23 Baked beans

24 The Polar Bear Club

25 c

26 So he can get men's eyeglass frames at no cost while getting rid of his ladies' glasses

27 a

28 A golf club

29 The "Lemon Tree" song (the Trini Lopez version)

30 "Tippy toe"

31 c

32 5A

33 David Letterman

34 c
35 Honolulu
36 b
37 A broom
38 c
39 Morty and Helen
40 c
41 The Coney Island auto pound to pick up his stolen car
42 a
43 A birthday party for his girlfriend's son
44 c
45 A student reporter for the NYU school newspaper
46 a (after she is bitten by one)
47 He hopes to bolster his status with his girlfriend by accompanying her to a funeral.
48 So Kramer can get bonus miles
49 A Polaroid of himself standing in front of the coffin
50 c
51 George (plotting revenge against his ex-boss)
52 a
53 A windshield
54 Ping
55 b
56 To end Sister Roberta's attraction to him
57 He wrestles away his girlfriend's Filofax.
58 c
59 Jerry's tax records for his IRS audit
60 a (George nicknames him Harry Fong.)
61 He gives his TV to George.
62 a

63 He holds the baby during the circumcision.

64 c

65 Soft cheeses

66 b

67 "Who's hungriest"

68 b

69 Corbin Bernson and George Wendt

70 *Jerry*

71 d

72 Jerry's accountant

73 b (Being with friends allows his date to see his relaxed, charming nondate personality.)

74 Books

75 Alton Benes

76 b

77 Mr. Costanza's old cabana shirt

78 c

79 The NBC president's fifteen-year-old daughter, Molly

80 c

81 A necklace

82 a

83 He ruins it by wearing it on a snowy evening

84 Robert Wagner

85 Elaine

86 Get a sample of Jerry's hair

87 b

88 a

89 George

90 The salt and pepper shakers

91 c

92 Crazy Joe Davola

93 c

94 A piece of pie

95 b

96 *TV Guide*s

97 c

98 c

99 He absentmindedly kisses her in front of her superiors.

100 a

101 Maple syrup

102 c

103 A Commando 8*

104 a

105 Queens College

106 Jerry

107 Marie

108 b (Kramer describes Jerry's substandard haircut as such, after Jerry's incompetent barber, Enzo)

109 Newman

110 b

111 Kramer

112 a

113 Quilt

114 d

115 d

116 *Rochelle, Rochelle*

117 a

118 To see their friends' baby

119 She works in Elaine's office.

120 d

121 A wooden Indian

122 Elaine

123 He literally bumps into a modeling agent who tells him that he has extraordinary hands.

124 d

125 His vacuum and attachments

126 c

127 George

128 Beltless

129 He has to go to the bathroom.

130 b

A.K.A.

1 d

2 b

3 a

4 c

5 d

6 a

7 d

8 b

9 d

New York, New York No. 2

1 c

2 g

3 d

4 i
5 j
6 b
7 a
8 e
9 f
10 h

Edibles, Too

1 h
2 c
3 g
4 j
5 a
6 f
7 i
8 e
9 b
10 d

LEVEL 4

1 b
2 Pete's Luncheonette
3 a
4 b
5 Vandelay Industries
6 b

7 b

8 Elaine

9 Gino

10 a

11 Jujyfruits

12 c

13 Triangles

14 d

15 She's a mumbler. (Everything she says is inaudible.)

16 b

17 To cover his black eyes caused by a scuba-diving mishap

18 a

19 Elle Macpherson

20 c

21 His beloved jacket

22 c

23 Mangos (He compares their effect to getting a B_{12} shot.)

24 George (reassuring an employer about his qualifications)

25 b and c (Elaine describes it as "Epstein-Barr with a twist of Lyme.")

26 She rolled over on a tick while doing the love-in scene during the production of *Hair* in Danbury, Connecticut.

27 He unknowingly contributes to a fraudulent charity.

28 a

29 Isosceles

30 b

31 The New York Health Club

32 d

33 She's afraid she'll be left out of the conversation.

34 b

35 His birthday

36 b

37 Queens

38 d

39 Because Jerry goes to the barber's nephew for a haircut

40 b

41 Rudy's Antique Boutique

42 b

43 He hears an erotic tape-recorded message she jokingly leaves for Jerry.

44 His mother (Her former boyfriend left it at her apartment.)

45 Paella

46 a

47 He's constantly sniffing.

48 c

49 a

50 In gym class at school. (Jerry was spotting George while he was climbing a rope.)

51 Pendant Publishing (where Elaine is assigned to work on it)

52 c (He last vomited on 6-29-80.)

53 Joel Rifkin

54 c

55 His goal is to have over 360 pairs so he only has to do wash once a year.

56 *The Coffee Table Book of Coffee Tables*

57 d

58 He shatters a glass and a shard hits the director.

59 c

60 His keys are left in the car by the neighborhood car parker

61 c

62 She slips and falls upon catching George masturbating.

63 b

64 He and Kramer attempt to put concrete in one of the laundromat's washing machines.

65 d

66 a (This required city dwellers to wear name tags to make the city a friendlier place. The failure of this suggestion was dubbed the "name tag fiasco.")

67 Lewis

68 Hennigan's (Kramer dubs it the "no-smell, no-tell scotch.")

69 a

70 For falling over the railing at a Yankees game after getting beaned by a foul ball

71 b

72 The network president disappears and his successor cancels it.

73 c

74 7½

75 A company that has developed a new technique for televising opera

76 An ulcer test

77 b

78 A sitcom writer and an actor (He played himself.)

79 d

80 Elaine (when she considers renting Jerry's apartment)

81 c

82 c

83 George (who supposedly can squint his way down to 20/30 vision)

84 b (because the driver would be up on the stage and wouldn't talk to her)

85 In his high-school gym teacher's possession

86 b

87 Mr. Lippman

88 b

89 Tina

90 Kramer can't remember where he parked.

91 b

92 "Kavorka" (A priest tells Kramer it means the "lure of the animal" and explains Sister Roberta's attraction to him.)

93 a

94 For her ability to fake orgasms

95 Uncle Leo

96 c

97 A bouquet of paper flowers made from the *TV Guide* she leaves on the subway

98 Nickelodeon

99 c

100 JFK High School

101 a

102 b

103 He gives the car away to a bum on the street.

104 c

105 His high-school gym teacher

106 a

107 Elaine

108 a

109 40 short

110 a

111 c

112 A Chinese restaurant

113 b

114 The kitchen

115 a

116 *Guys and Dolls*

117 b

118 c

119 He moves back home with his parents.

120 Mice

121 a

122 He tells her about the masturbation competition.

123 a

124 c

125 To literally get even with the cashier who he believes had previously shortchanged him

126 c

127 Rubberman

128 b

129 Prell

130 b

New York, New York No. 3

1 d
2 i
3 b
4 g
5 c
6 h
7 f
8 e
9 j
10 a

More Potpourri

1 a
2 b
3 a
4 d
5 e
6 c
7 b
8 b

LEVEL 5

1 129 W. 81st Street
2 The Aryan Union
3 Elaine's subway admirer, Ricky
4 His real-life nephew

5 1409

6 A company that is designing a robot butcher

7 Bob Sacamano

8 Rick Barr Properties

9 Yoo-Hoo

10 555-8643

11 a

12 b

13 Jerry Seinfeld

14 Tweety Bird

15 *Fair Game*

16 Uromysitisis poisoning

17 145 (After taking George's IQ test, her score goes up to 151.)

18 Culottes

19 The Klapdo D-29*

20 St. Louis

21 Donald

22 A chain of make-your-own pizza restaurants

23 A horse

24 Keith Hernandez

25 Green

26 Volcano relief fund for Krakatoa

27 A Macintosh PowerBook Duo that replaced a Macintosh SE from earlier episodes

28 Sentrax*

29 Volume 41, Number 31

30 *The Keys*

ABOUT THE AUTHOR

Beth B. Golub is an attorney who lives in a northern suburb of Chicago with her husband. She loves chocolate babkas.